HELP!
I'M BEING DEPLOYED

Barrett Craig

Consulting Editor: Dr. Paul Tautges

© 2014 by Barrett Craig

ISBN
Paper: 978-1-63342-000-7
ePub: 978-1-63342-001-4
Kindle: 978-1-63342-002-1

Shepherd Press
P.O. Box 24
Wapwallopen, PA 18660

www.shepherdpress.com

First printed by Day One Publications

Designed by **documen**

CONTENTS

Introduction   4

1 What Makes Deployment so Difficult   7

2 Why Deployments?   12

3 The Hope in Deployment   25

4 Glorifying God While Deployed   43

   Conclusion   56

   Personal Application Projects   57

   Where Can I Get More Help?   62

INTRODUCTION

"**P**ack your gear up tonight, PFC Craig; we're leaving for Kuwait tomorrow!" Those were the words I heard from my squad leader on my answering machine after returning home from a night of fun with my friends. My heartbeat immediately kicked in to high gear. I was excited. I was scared. I was slightly in shock. All my training as a marine had led to this moment.

I entered boot camp in August 1996. At the ripe age of eighteen, I stood on the infamous yellow footprints, met my Drill Instructor, and my life changed forever. As military members know, D.I.s train us in every aspect of military life. On one occasion, in an attempt to prepare us for how suddenly deployments might come, our D.I.s played a mean, but plausible, joke on us.

They began a class by showing us a sobering documentary of recent past wars and the young men and women like ourselves who had fought.

The documentary showed the hardships of war, the harsh conditions, and the pain of combat etched on the soldiers' faces. As the reality of deployments and war began to hit home, one D.I. quickly ran in, flipped on the lights, turned the video off, and said, "Listen up, recruits. We have a situation on our hands. We've just got word that things have got hot again in the Middle East. Your presence is needed immediately in support of a combat operation. Your time here in boot camp will be cut short by three weeks, and you will report directly to Marine Combat Training School for three weeks of intensive infantry training, after which you'll immediately be shipped overseas." My heart started to race and my palms began to sweat. What did this mean?

Our D.I.s let us squirm and sweat a little before they admitted to their mean little joke. As a loud sigh of relief echoed around the room, they laughed. We learned our lesson: deployments come suddenly, and we have to be ready.

Sixteen years later, now as a chaplain, and having deployed numerous times to numerous countries, I still feel the whole mixture of emotions when I leave: excitement, fear, anxiety, loneliness, panic, uncertainty, grief (leaving family and friends), anger, frustration, and even joy. Deployment is still hard.

You may be reading this booklet in preparation for your first deployment. You may have already accomplished several deployments. Or perhaps you are a spouse, parent, or even the child of a deployed military member. Regardless of your situation, it is my desire in these few short chapters to prepare you for deployment, to provide a biblical framework and strategies to help you successfully navigate through it while walking faithfully with Christ, and to help you to rest in the gospel, to finish well, and to do it all to the glory of God.

1

What Makes Deployment So Difficult?

Aren't the difficulties of deployments self-evident? We don't need to point out the obvious. We're away from those we know, living in a foreign land, and working long days in difficult conditions. Deployments are just hard.

When we train for battle, the military tries to create worst-case scenarios or a difficult environment here at home in order to prepare us for the real thing abroad. As is often said in the military, "To be prepared is half the victory," and soldiers must be prepared for the difficulties. That's why we train when it rains, through the night, without food, with heavy gear on—and we do it all over again. We attempt to foresee every possible scenario and prepare for it.

In the same way, we as Christians must plan for the spiritual difficulties that may lie ahead. We must prepare and think through them in order that when those difficulties come, they won't be as surprising and hard. Yes, some of the spiritual difficulties of deployment are self-evident, but not all. Either way, whether we are seasoned in deploying or new to deployment, we can always prepare ourselves better spiritually for the difficulties that may come. Think through the following hardships you may face.

The Spiritual Difficulties of Separation

When the brow of the ship is raised or the airplane takes off, the shock of separation will be inevitable. Be prepared for these:

»   Separation from your familiar and safe vironment, such as your own home, your familiar neighbors, your neighborhood

»   Separation from your regular routines and special events, such as the coffee shop you hang out at or the holiday parties you always attend, and maybe even family birthdays

»   Separation from friends and family, the ones who are closest to you, those whom you lean on and love, and around whom you can be yourself

»   Separation from your church, Sunday ministry, your pastor asking "How are you doing?," and fellow church members taking you out to lunch and making you laugh.

The Spiritual Difficulties of the Unknown

While on my most recent deployment, I had the privilege of participating in the "Crossing the Line Ceremony." This is a time-honored Naval tradition whereby the Sailor or Marine who has yet to cross below the equator must undergo an initiation rite in which he or she is "cleansed" from being a Pollywog so as to become a Shellback.

You might be asking yourself at this point, "What does that mean?" As a newly appointed Shellback, I'm sworn to secrecy about the ceremony so as to provoke fear in all future Pollywogs. (But I can assure worried mothers that the ceremony was done very tastefully and safely, and is good fun.)

But what makes the Crossing the Line Ceremony so difficult? It is the fear of the unknown, the same thing that makes deployments so difficult. Where will I go during my deployment? When will I return? What will my living conditions be like? Will I have any Christian friends? What will I eat? Will I be able to make contact with my family? Will I cope? What will our days look like? Will I have to fight? Will I get injured? Will I die? Will my buddy die? The list goes on, and the questions invariably become more difficult.

The Spiritual Difficulties of the Military Environment

When on deployment, especially in a combat zone, your whole soul and body are constantly on the alert. What's going to happen? Where's my rifle? Where are the exits? Where can I find cover? Am I ready? The military environment on deployment, whether in a chopper, in a plane, on a ship, or on the land, is intense. Everyone is on edge. After all, life and death are in the balance.

At this point, you may have begun devising a plan to avoid your deployment altogether! Deployments are hard! I understand. Yes, there are innumerable things that make deployments great too, but you must be prepared when these various spiritual difficulties come. I want you especially to be prepared with the knowledge that the Lord is very kind to his children, and if you are a believer, you should expect nothing less. He's got you. He really does. That's why I want you to keep reading.

2

Why Deployments?

Ponder these questions: Why do we have to leave the comfort of our homes and friendships to go to a foreign land? Why do we have to leave our crying spouses and children behind? Why do we have to suffer the difficult types of living conditions we often face in foreign countries? Why the hardship? Why the sadness, loneliness, and homesickness? Even more, why war, death, and destruction? Why? Is there something bigger going on than merely our own national interests? Why ultimately are there deployments in the first place?.

Does the Bible have an answer? It does. And for the Christian in the military, understanding what the Bible has to say about the world and its condition is crucial for rightly understanding not only what's wrong with the world, but also why deployments exist and are, in fact, necessary. The Bible gives us two overarching reasons why deployments exist—a spiritual reason and a practical reason.

A Spiritual Reason: What's Wrong with Us?

What's wrong with the world? Why do people treat one another the way they do? Why is it broken? Why all the pain? Why all the heartache? What happened? Where did it all go wrong? It all began in the Garden of Eden in the very beginning.

GOD'S GOOD CREATION

> *In the beginning God created the heavens and the earth ... And God said, "Let there be light," and there was light.*
>
> *(Genesis 1:1, 3)*

What power! What wisdom! Speaking the universe into existence out of nothing! In fact, in six days, God added more variety, more detail, and more beauty. Then, like a master artist, God stood back, looked at his creation, and said, "This is good!"

But God wasn't finished. One last touch was needed, one last act whereby he created someone to uniquely bear his image and likeness—man. "Male and female he created them" (Genesis 1:27). He again looked at all he created and said, "This is very good!" No evil, no pain, no death—and no deployments! Then on the seventh day, he rested from his creative work.

The Warning

God graciously gave the Garden of Eden to Adam and Eve to enjoy. They were to be its caretakers, to develop it, partake of all its fruit, populate it with children, and delight in it with God. God in his goodness also put a glorious tree in the middle of the garden and named it the Tree of the Knowledge of Good and Evil. The tree was a gentle reminder that the garden, the world—everything—belonged to God. God was the ultimate King of both the garden and of man (Genesis 2:16–17).

How good God was to them! He gave them everything in the garden to eat, forbidding them to eat from only one of those trees. God's command not to eat of that tree signified that he is our Creator and our Lord, and we are to obey him. It also demonstrated that God would take care of Adam, Eve, and their offspring; he would provide for them, protect them, and safely lead them; he would grow them in knowledge and wisdom by their abstaining from eating from that tree; and he knew what was best for them. It meant that there is nothing in all the world more satisfying than God.

The Fall

As God was creating the material world we enjoy, he was also, behind the scenes, creating something else. He created a majestic immaterial realm full of dazzling angels whom God would employ to serve him for the sake of his people. Yet something terrible happened in heaven after God declared all things good. One of those angels, named Lucifer, now known as Satan, led a host of other angels to rebel against God and his glorious reign—a foolish endeavor. Yet in quick fashion, God cast Satan and his demons out of heaven and away from his presence (see 2 Peter 2:4; Jude 6). But Satan's rebellion did not end there. He immediately went to work to deceive and persuade Adam and Eve to rebel, too!

Satan, disguised as a serpent, cast doubt on God's word by asking Eve, "Did God actually say ...?" and he tempted her to eat from the tree (Genesis 3:1–5). Tragically, the worst happened: Adam and Eve sinned (Genesis 3:6). Desiring to be independent of God, they rebelled against his command. Through one small bite, one seemingly small act of disobedience—believing a lie instead of the truth—Adam and Eve were suddenly cut off from the privileged face-to-face relationship they had enjoyed with God.

Present-Day Implications

"What does Adam and Eve's rebellion have to do with deployments? How is this information relevant?" you may be thinking. It has everything to do with deployments. Adam and Eve's rebellion didn't end there, and, in fact, it has never ended; it only escalated, becoming increasingly vile and wicked. They passed their rebellion on to their children and through them to all mankind:

> ... Sin came into the world through one man, and death through sin, and so death spread to all men because all sinned ...
>
> (Romans 5:12)

The Bible says that all men and women have gone astray;

> we have turned—every one—to his own way.
>
> (Isaiah 53:6)

We disobey God through murder, greed, sexual immorality, theft, covetousness, pride, the pursuit of power, and living our lives the way we think best rather than submitting to God's good laws. We have a huge spiritual problem. And so the world is the way it is—an ugly mess ... and full of deployments.

A Practical Reason: God's Continued Command to Love and Protect

The Bible also gives a second, practical reason why we must go on deployments. Despite our living in a fallen world, God commands us all to love one another and protect the innocent from evil people:

> *Keep far from a false charge, and do not kill the innocent and righteous, for I will not acquit the wicked.*
>
> *(Exodus 23:7)*

> *You shall not take vengeance or bear a grudge against the sons of your own people, but you shall love your neighbour as yourself: I am the Lord.*
>
> *(Leviticus 19:18)*

In fact, the command to love our neighbour is second only to the greatest command:

> *One of [the Pharisees], a lawyer, asked*

him a question to test him. "Teacher,
which is the great commandment in the
Law?" And he said to him, "You shall love
the Lord your God with all your heart and
with all your soul and with all your mind."
This is the great and first commandment.
And a second is like it: You shall love
your neighbour as yourself. On these two
commandments depend all the Law and
the Prophets.

(Matthew 22:35–40;
see also Deuteronomy 6:5; Luke 10:26–27)

So, what does it mean to love our neighbour and
protect the innocent? Does it mean possibly
having to kill another person? Does it mean
war? Below is a basic understanding of what the
Bible says about why the military exists and why
deployments are necessary.

Living In Between the Garden and Heaven

When we consider war, there is a conundrum
Christians must first embrace. As we have seen,
the Bible says that no one is righteous (that is, all
men and women are sinners; see Romans 3:10–12),
and so in our world we have murder, war, greed,

sexual immorality, covetousness, ungodly pursuits of power, and so on.

At the same time, we also read in the Bible that God has a plan whereby he will ultimately eradicate evil and reverse what Adam and Eve did in the garden. He will create a new heaven and earth (Revelation 21:1–4). We know the end of the story, where God is guiding all history.

However, heaven has not yet come; we are, in a sense, living in between the garden and heaven. While we are assured of, and await, the Lord's return and ultimate restoration in the new heaven and new earth, we still live in a post-garden world that is devastated by evil men and women who rebel against God—including you and me! But when Adam and Eve rebelled against God in the garden, severing their relationship with him, God did not give them—or us—license for further disobedience. No; God gave us further commands to follow, and these continuing commands are still summed up in the two greatest commandments we looked at above: to love the Lord our God with all our heart, soul, and might, and to love our neighbour as ourselves.

When we correctly understand how God wants us to love him and our neighbour, we learn that

God oftentimes deals out consequences in the here and now for those who unjustly treat their neighbor. Sometimes the consequence for the injustice is physical death—even through the activity of war.

The Legitimacy of the Death Penalty

In Genesis 6, we read of wickedness increasing in the world. Unspeakable evil was taking place and God's rage was kindled. As a result, God commanded Noah to build an ark for him and his family because God was going to eradicate the population of the wicked on the earth through a flood (Genesis 6–8).

It is important to observe from the flood account that God did not turn a blind eye to the evil activity. Instead, he dealt out consequences for evil actions. In fact, these consequences were far more severe than anything that had gone before. He flooded the whole earth, physically killing every person except Noah and his family. God personally administered the death penalty to wicked people. Interestingly, when we continue to read into Genesis 9, after the flood subsided and Noah and his family disembarked from the ark, we find a very important new command given to Noah and the generations that followed. God said,

> *Whoever sheds the blood of man, by man*
> *shall his blood be shed, for God made*
> *man in his own image.*
> (Genesis 9:6)

God passed to us the responsibility for administering the death penalty on his behalf. God gave permission and authority to mankind to kill a person who had murdered another person. The reason why God made death the penalty for murder is because of the incredible value man has, having been made in God's image. Executing a murderer shows how much God values life— which means that administering the death penalty is a good and godly activity when carried out appropriately by the governing authorities who "bear the sword" (Romans 13:4).

The Legitimacy of a Government

God's command to administer the death penalty doesn't mean he gives individuals permission to be vigilantes who can kill murderers on their own. Rather, as we continue reading on in the Old Testament, especially in the books of Exodus, Leviticus, and Deuteronomy, we see God putting the ultimate authority to administer judgments, including the death penalty, in the hands of Israel's governmental authorities (Deuteronomy 17:8-20). But this was not just an Old Testament idea. In fact, as we move into the New Testament, God is even clearer in his Word about his purpose for governmental authorities to bear the responsibility of upholding justice among their people:

> Be subject for the Lord's sake to every
> human institution, whether it be to the
> emperor as supreme, or to governors as
> sent by him to punish those who do evil
> and to praise those who do good.
> (1 Peter 2:13-14; see also Romans 13:1-4)

The Legitimacy of War

According to the Old and New Testaments, every nation has been called to obey God's overall mandate to uphold justice, protect the innocent, and care for its people—following the overarching command to love our neighbor.

But what does loving our neighbor have to do with war? Let's think of it on a smaller scale. If you happened to be out with one of your friends and you noticed a young woman being attacked by a thug in an alley, your military training would kick in and you would both run to rescue the woman and subdue the thug. If the thug had a knife and threatened you, you would presumably seek to injure him severely, maybe even to the point of death, to keep him from hurting you and, most importantly, the young woman. Your actions are prompted by love.

War is this type of love seen on a grand scale. When a nation, then, is being unjustly attacked by another nation, and this attacking nation is murdering innocent people for unjust gain, the governmental authorities of the nation being attacked have a responsibility under God's authority to protect the innocent by defending themselves and subduing, even killing, the murderous attackers.

If you are a military member of the United States, it might be helpful for you to know that the USA generally uses the following just-war guidelines, which in many ways are biblical, when considering whether or not to engage in a war:

»   Are Americans or our allies in real danger for their lives?

»   Are our actions to go to war equal with the offense of the evil actions of the other nation?

» Are our governmental authorities in areement (at least a majority) to go to war?

» Do we have good intentions?

» Do we think we can win?

» Is going to war our last resort?

» Do the benefits of winning a war against the nation outweigh letting that nation continue its evil activity?

Let me add one more comment. If you ever find yourself in a situation where you think that you are given an order to kill an innocent person or treat someone inhumanely, or carry out any other morally questionable act, be sure to seek out help, whether from a leader, a fellow soldier, or even a chaplain.

The Legitimacy of the Soldier

Over and over again in the Bible we see God favoring and blessing the work of those in the military. In fact, the warrior King David blessed God saying,

> Blessed be the Lord, my rock, who
> trains my hands for war, and my fingers
> for battle.
>
> (Psalm 144:1–2)

Even in the New Testament, soldiers are many times praised and never discouraged from continuing in their military service (Matthew 8:5–10; Acts 10:6, 22; Philippians 1:13; 2 Timothy 2:4). Simply stated, God affirms your position as a soldier. He is with you in your work.

Be confident in your job. You fulfill an important role in the hand of God for the sake of good, for the sake of the protection and freedom of innocent people from evil men, and for the sake of God's glory. If you are called to a situation in which you are directed to "pull the trigger," you can confidently know that you have God's blessing on your activity. You are God's agent for love.

A Glimmer of Hope in the Midst of the Spiritual and Practical Mess of Deployments

With all this talk of the spiritual disorder in the world and the mess of wars, life might still look a little bleak right now. You may be asking if there is any ultimate hope. Is there any hope in your deployment? Can any good come from it? Will there ever be a day when deployments don't exist? Well, the answer to all these questions is "Yes!"

3 The Hope in Deployment

When I was in the Philippines, I had the opportunity of watching a routine practice flight for some military aircraft in the region. A few marines and I, while perched on a lookout, were enjoying the view of the Philippine jungle before the sky began to turn dark as the sun tucked down below the horizon. In the distance, we saw the glimmer of a C-130 coming toward us and flying close above the dense, tropical hills below. To our surprise, out from the back of the plane shot several flares into the dusky sky, lighting up the ground beneath. It was spectacular. The brightness swept the darkness of the night sky away and we could see the trees below.

Having read the previous couple of chapters, you may be gazing upon life just as we initially gazed upon an otherwise beautiful view going dark as the sun fell below the horizon. The picture that the Bible has painted for us is of a dark and fallen world where sin reigns, men and women are estranged from God, and we face wars, deployments, and pain.

But the story isn't over yet. There is a bright hope on the horizon. There is a more glorious light that has come, a more glorious hope. It is the hope of One who, like a flare in the night sky, has flooded the darkness with rays of light, rescuing us from all the sin and brokenness of this world. The light, the hope, is Jesus Christ.

The Hope for the World

Jesus was no ordinary man. As we read of his life and ministry in the Gospels of Matthew, Mark, Luke, and John, we read not of a man who simply went around doing good things, but of a man with a miraculous record. Jesus fulfilled numerous prophecies (Luke 4:21); he was miraculously conceived (Matthew 1:20); he performed many miracles (John 12:37; 20:30); and he demonstrated his power over physical health (Matthew 8:16), weather patterns (Mark 4:39), the laws of physics (Matthew 14:26), the demonic world (Luke 11:20), and death (John 11:43–44)!

Jesus claimed to be the very Son of God (Luke 9:20–21), always obeying God his Father and living a perfect, sinless life (1 Peter 2:22). He spoke with authority (Matthew 7:29), claimed to be truth incarnate (John 14:6), and proved his claim to authority by accomplishing unquestionably the greatest miracle of all, dying a gruesome death and then gloriously rising from the dead (Matthew 28:6).

But what was all this for? Why did he come? What did he accomplish? He accomplished what the Bible calls "the gospel."

What Does Christ Have To Do with Me?

The truth of the matter is that, ultimately, you and I do not need rescuing from any upcoming deployment; we need rescuing from our sin—to be brought back into a right relationship with the God of the universe, our Creator. The greatest war is not between nation and nation, it's between us and God—and we're the ones who need to surrender!

The Gospel

"Gospel" means good news. We know what it is to receive good news. We love and long for it, but the good news that surpasses all other good news is Jesus and what he offers.

Imagine if you owed $1 million through frivolous

spending and were in big trouble, and then a wealthy man came along and said, "I want to pay all your debt; then I want to credit to your account $1 billion, so that you'll never have any financial problems ever again." Now that would be good news!

In Jesus Christ, God offers us a deal whereby Jesus will pay the debt of our sin, then credit to us the wealth of his righteousness to guarantee everlasting life with him in heaven. And it's all free! This is how it works.

God Is Holy

Over and over again in the Bible we read of God's holiness; for example,

> *Holy, holy, holy is the Lord of hosts;*
> *the whole earth is full of his glory!*
> (Isaiah 6:3)

That God is holy means that he is totally separated from sin and from doing wrong things. He does not commit sin, he does not join in with sin, and he does not even flirt with anything that might be conveyed as sin. Furthermore, he cannot be in a relationship with someone who breaks his laws, even a little:

For whoever keeps the whole law but fails in one point has become accountable for all of it.

(James 2:10)

That God is holy also means that he is totally committed to doing what is right. Everything that God does is right. His motives are right, his thoughts are right, and his actions are right. There is no one like him. He is perfect (Matthew 5:48), and we are not.

We Are Rebels

Not only does the Bible clearly testify about the reality of our sin nature (Romans 3:23), but also your experience up to this point in your life should make it very clear that you—and I—have not loved God with all your heart, soul, and mind, and loved your neighbor as yourself. We are rebels, too. Perhaps you have not done the types of wicked things others have done, but, nonetheless, our records are tainted in some way—whether by mean things we have said, things we have stolen from others, times we have lied or cheated, ungodly relationships we should have avoided, or images we should not have looked at. We fall short.

What We Deserve

Jesus spoke more on the subject of eternal death than any other biblical author. He characterized eternal death, what he called "hell," as a place of "outer darkness" (Matthew 8:12), with "eternal fire" (Matthew 25:41), and where the pain of torment will never go away (Matthew 22:13)—ever (Revelation 14:11). Hell is where God pours out his judgment, his wrath, on rebels for eternity. This is a very sobering reality. In fact, if you learn anything about hell, it's that it highlights how much displeasure God has toward sin, our rebellion, and our disobedience. He does not tolerate it. He will judge us for it forever, unless someone saves us from that judgment.

What Christ Has Done

Christ is where we see God's unfathomable wisdom and his amazing grace. What Christ accomplished through his life, death, and resurrection is how God is able to remain just in his holiness, yet entirely forgive us of our disobedience (Romans 3:26).

Christ is qualified to bring us back into a right relationship with God because he is perfectly holy. Jesus is the only one who has obeyed God's laws perfectly; he never rebelled or disobeyed (1 Peter 2:22). Therefore, he is a qualified substitute for us (Romans 3:24–25). When Christ willingly went to the cross, he went in the place of sinners. In other words, he took the wrath of God, the death penalty, on himself in our place.

> For our sake [God] made him to be sin
> who knew no sin, so that in him we might
> become the righteousness of God.
> (2 Corinthians 5:21)

What God has done in Christ is all-encompassing. Christ's death and resurrection not only satisfied God's wrath so that he could forgive us our sins, but they also enabled God to credit Christ's perfect holiness, his righteousness, to our account on the basis of faith (Isaiah 53:11; 2 Corinthians 5:21; Philippians 3:9). If we are in Christ, when God sees us, he does not see our tainted sinful record, but he sees Christ (Galatians 2:20). Now that's the best news!

Our Response to the Gospel

We have all in one way or another, to one degree or another, violated God's commands. We are all guilty. We must come to grips with the fact that we cannot earn God's acceptance by our merits or by living out our definition of a good life. If we are to be saved, we must respond properly to Christ and what he has done. What is a proper response? Jesus communicated this best when he said, Repent and believe in the gospel (Mark 1:15).

Repent

The word "repent" does not have the most welcoming sound. It simply means to turn away from sin, yet when many hear this word, they feel judged or not understood. But when Jesus says it, he is not standing from above, pointing his finger down toward us in accusation. Rather, he is pleading with us in desperation to save our lives. When Jesus is saying "repent," he is not trying to take something good from you, he is trying to give you something better—himself, eternal life! In other word, repentance is a good thing!

What, then, is Jesus calling us to repent from? From living lives of disobedience against his good and holy commands; of not loving God with all our heart, soul, and mind; of not loving our neighbor as ourselves; of living lives of stealing, lying, adultery, murder, hatred, covetousness, and of dishonoring authorities—and all this both in our actions and in our hearts. Jesus is saying that we must repent from the rebellious, sinful, and destructive path we are going down and which leads to death, and come to life, to true happiness and satisfaction, that is found only in Christ. Jesus is ultimately saying that we need to turn from the misery of our sin to the only God in whose presence there is fullness of joy and pleasures forevermore (Psalm 16:11). What a glorious alternative!

Believe

But Christ does not want us, upon repenting, to just stop going in a sinful direction. Jesus says we must "believe"! The type of believing Jesus is talking about here and throughout the New Testament is not merely affirming that he was a real person in history, like believing that General Douglas MacArthur was a real military figure who played a key role in World War II. Neither is it merely trusting that Jesus can help you out in a difficult situation, like asking a friend for a quick loan when you are in a bind. Rather, the type of believing Jesus has in mind is the kind of trust you put in a fellow soldier in battle to cover you while you run down range. Jesus is calling on us to trust him and him alone with our whole lives and to rescue us from the wrath of God we deserve.

Believe Him as Your Savior

When Jesus calls on us to trust him to save us, he wants us to come to him recognizing that we need a savior.

> *For God so loved the world, that he gave*
> *his only Son, that whoever believes in him*
> *should not perish but have eternal life.*
> *(John 3:16)*

We must come knowing that God is holy, that we have individually rebelled against him, and that our rebellion deserves his wrath—but that he, Jesus, having lived a perfect life, willingly went to the cross and rose from the dead, both to pay the punishment for our sin and to credit us with his holiness in order to make us right with God and enjoy him for eternity.

Believe Him as Your Lord

In addition, when Jesus calls on us to trust him to save us, he wants us to come to him recognizing that he is fully worthy of being followed. Jesus was very clear on this point. He said,

> If anyone would come after me, let him deny himself and take up his cross and follow me.
>
> (Mark 8:34)

Trusting Christ presupposes we are willing to follow him, obey him, and go with him the rest of our lives. And it's worth it!

If you have not already placed your faith in Jesus Christ for your salvation, I urge you to do so! Trust him! God's Word promises not only eternal life in the future, but abundant life here and now. As the Good Shepherd, Jesus said,

> I came that they may have life and have it abundantly.
>
> (John 10:10)

I assure you that it's worth it. The countless military men and women I have had the pleasure of serving and who have basked in their newfound relationship with the God of the universe say it's worth it, too. Please, trust in Jesus.

What We Receive upon Our Response: All God's Promises

Once we respond to Jesus by trusting in him, what we receive is far greater than anything we have ever received or achieved before—and I can assure you that it even makes hope in our deployments possible. Yes, the greatest hope in deployment is having Christ, being in a right relationship with him, and no longer being God's enemy but his friend. Yet God gives us so much more! Consider the following promises we have in Christ:

» Eternal life: "Whoever believes in the Son has eternal life" (John 3:36).

» The Spirit: "Because you are sons, God has sent the Spirit of his Son into our hearts, crying, 'Abba! Father!'" (Galatians 4:6; see also Ephesians 1:13).

» Forgiveness of sins and being made righteous: "For our sake he made him to be sin who knew no sin, so that in him we might become the righteousness of God" (2 Corinthians 5:21).

» Adoption as his sons: "You have received the Spirit of adoption as sons, by whom we cry, 'Abba! Father!'" (Romans 8:15).

» He will never leave or forsake you: "He has said, 'I will never leave you nor forsake you'" (Hebrews 13:5).

» He will work all things together for your good: "We know that for those who love God all things work together for good, for those who are called according to his purpose" (Romans 8:28).

» He will hear your prayers: "Ask, and it will be given to you; seek, and you will find; knock, and it will be opened to you. For everyone who asks receives, and the one who seeks finds, and to the one who knocks it will be opened" (Matthew 7:7–8).

» He will love you: "In this is love, not that we have loved God but that he loved us and sent his Son to be the propitiation for our sins" (1 John 4:10).

And there is so much more! God gives us every good thing that he possibly has to give (Ephesians 1:3). Embracing and latching on to all these promises God has given you in Christ is genuinely the secret to living a happy and thriving Christian life—especially on deployment.

Why the Gospel Must Remain Central to Our Lives and Our Deployment

The gospel, the good news of Jesus Christ's sin-atoning death, burial, and glorious resurrection on our behalf, is the most important thing for Christians (new and old) to grasp. As believers in Christ, we have the tendency either to add to what Christ has already done for us, by trying to make God accept us on the basis of the good things we do (Galatians 3:2), or to think that as we are forgiven and made holy, we can live however we want to live (1 Corinthians 5:1–2). When we read through the New Testament, we see both extremes.

However, the Bible teaches us that as Christians, we are to rest in the gospel, enjoying God's acceptance of us through Christ alone while joyfully obeying God's commands because they are best for us, bringing us happiness and training us in holiness. In fact, when you read through many of the New Testament letters, you will often find the authors spending the first half of their letters explaining the gospel to those who are already Christians, and the second half explaining the type of life that should be produced from that gospel (compare Romans 1–11 with 12–16; and Ephesians 1–3 with 4–6). So, as Christians, we must go back to the gospel over and over again to remind ourselves what God in Christ has rescued us from—sin—and what he has rescued us to—a life of holiness.

I like to think of the gospel as it relates to the Christian life using the following three metaphors: foundation, framework, and fountainhead.

The Gospel Is the Foundation of Our Ultimate Hope

Every good Seabee or Combat Engineer knows that the success of a structure is contingent upon having a good foundation. Often, the foundation takes the longest time to build, because of the need to ensure that the soil is tamped down, level, and secure before pouring on the concrete. If the foundation is faulty, the structure is doomed to fall. In the same way, the gospel must be what you stand on; it must be your foundation. When you begin standing on your own strength, relying on your own goodness, or resting in your own skills and talents, your joy and stability in your walk with God will fall. Jesus is clear:

> I am the vine; you are the branches.
> Whoever abides in me and I in him, he
> it is that bears much fruit, for apart from

me you can do nothing.

(John 15:5)

The Gospel Is the Framework Out of Which We Grow in Godliness

As Christians, God now calls us to
Be holy in all your conduct.

(1 Peter 1:15)

He calls us to grow in righteousness, aligning our thoughts, motives, actions, goals, and purposes with his. But, as stated above, our tendency is to trust in Christ for salvation and then begin to pursue holiness in order to win God's approval. In other words, Christians often try to construct their own framework of a righteous life on the foundation of the gospel, rather than resting in the framework of the righteousness Christ has already constructed for us. To strive to win God's approval by our own good deeds ultimately diminishes everything that Jesus did for us on the cross. Remember, Jesus won God's approval for us! So, as we seek to follow God, growing in godliness, turning from our sin and obeying his good commands, we must do it on the basis of knowing that God in Christ has already declared us righteous (Romans 8:1–4).

The Gospel Is the Fountainhead from Which We Live Our Lives

The Bible repeatedly calls us to love the Lord with all our heart, to rejoice in the Lord, and to walk with him in sincerity (Mark 12:30; Philippians 4:4; 1 Thessalonians 4:1). But what in fact makes God so worthy of our love, our rejoicing, and our fellowship? It's all that God has done in the gospel, through Jesus Christ!

> *In this is love, not that we have loved God but that he loved us and sent his Son to be the propitiation for our sins.*
>
> *(1 John 4:10)*

God wants us to be affected down in the deepest recesses of our hearts by what he has accomplished for us, so that our lives are an overflow of amazement in the gospel.

There Is Hope in Deployment

There is an enormous amount of hope in deployment for us as believers! We have the absolute expectation of all the promises of the gospel. Can it get any better than that? In fact, we genuinely have everything we need to accomplish our deployment. Why? Because ultimately, through the gospel, we have God! What a tremendous comfort!

But now we must take this great hope and work our deployment well, to the glory of God. God didn't save us to lie in our rack and play video games. He saved us to shine the light of his gospel to the world. He saved us to be his ambassadors (2 Corinthians 5:20).

4

Glorifying God While Deployed

As already mentioned, during your deployment you will face many challenges. But in so far as you keep the basics of the Christian life, resting in the gospel of Christ, your deployment will not only be more manageable to handle, it will also glorify and honor God.

1. Remember That God Is Doing Something Bigger

God Is About His Glory

The greatest task God has given us is to bring him glory (Isaiah 43:7). God has created and called us to glorify him.

> So, whether you eat or drink, or whatever you do, do all to the glory of God.
> (1 Corinthians 10:31)

What does the Bible mean by glorifying God? To

give glory simply means to point to something and give it recognition and honor, highlighting its worth. Thus, when we give glory to God, we live in such a way that our lives point to how great he is and what he has accomplished for us through Jesus Christ.

> Let your light shine before others, so that
> they may see your good works and give
> glory to your Father who is in heaven.
>
> (Matthew 5:16)

GOD IS IN CONTROL

We have a saying in the military: "It is what it is." In other words, you can't really do anything about a given situation; you just have to accept it. As a Christian, I understand the innocent meaning behind the statement, but I avoid saying it because I think it subtly denies God's control over all events.

The Bible is very clear that God is in control of all things:

> [He] works all things according to the
> counsel of his will
>
> (Ephesians 1:11)

*Whatever the Lord pleases, he does, in
heaven and on earth, in the seas and
all deeps.*

(Psalm 135:6)

Even when it comes to wars or natural disasters,
God is in control (Isaiah 45:7).

God Is Advancing His Kingdom

The best way to think about God's kingdom is to
remember what it was like in Eden before Adam
and Eve disobeyed, or to reflect on what heaven
will be like when God destroys this sinful world.
His kingdom will be a place where his people
are once again in a face-to-face relationship
with him, walking righteously, and willingly and
joyfully submitting to him as their good King
(Revelation 21).

All history, everything God is doing, is leading
to heaven, where we will fully experience his
kingdom. How is he advancing his kingdom?
Through massive military battles and strategic
foreign alliances? No. God is advancing his
kingdom through the Spirit, by saving the lost
and sanctifying his children.

HE IS SAVING THE LOST

Before Jesus ascended into heaven, he commissioned his disciples, you and me:

> Go therefore and make disciples of all nations, baptizing them in the name of the Father and of the Son and of the Holy Spirit, teaching them to observe all that I have commanded you. And behold, I am with you always, to the end of the age.
> (Matthew 28:19–20)

Jesus, by the Spirit, commands us to go and tell this great news of what Christ has accomplished. God's kingdom advances by our making the gospel known to the lost. Among the many things God has planned for you on your deployment, sharing the gospel with your fellow soldiers is one of them.

HE IS SANCTIFYING HIS CHILDREN

Often, one of the most difficult things for Christians to embrace is that God sanctifies us most commonly in trials, through producing "endurance" or "steadfastness" in us (Romans 5:2–5; James 1:2–4). When we think of trials, we often think of someone making fun of our faith or unjustly accusing us of something. But deployments are a form of suffering, too! All the challenges that come with deployment—small living quarters, injuries, long working hours, little or no communication with those at home, even war—God is using to conform your heart, motives, life, and goal to that of Jesus (2 Corinthians 3:18).

2. Strive to Maintain Basic Spiritual Disciplines

Military members know something about discipline. Discipline is the fundamental goal of our various branches' boot camps. Well, God calls us to discipline, too. The type of discipline he calls us to have is not the kind it takes to tread water for an hour or fight sleep while on post. Rather, it is the type that keeps us in close fellowship with God, his people, and his purposes (1 Timothy 4:7). Here are a few important disciplines to keep while on deployment.

KEEP GOD'S WORD CENTRAL IN YOUR LIFE

Take with you your Bible (consider a good study Bible), then, when on deployment, saturate your life with God's Word. A Bible-verse memory strategy, such as "Fighter Verses," would be an excellent resource. Jesus said,

*It is written, "Man shall not live by bread
alone, but by every word that comes from
the mouth of God."*

(Matthew 4:4)

Work hard to make God's Word part of your daily
schedule and life in the following ways:

» Read it (Psalm 19:7–8).

» Meditate on and memorize it (Psalm 1:1–2).

» Sing it (Psalm 135:3).

» Hear it preached (2 Timothy 4:1–3).

» Pray it (Matthew 6:9–13).

» Speak it to build up others (Ephesians 5:18–20).

*FIND FELLOWSHIP, ACCOUNTABILITY, AND DISCIPLESHIP
RELATIONSHIPS*

God has saved us into a family. And there are
thousands in the family of God in the military.
Look for fellowship. Look also for the opportunity
to teach a younger Christian about walking with
Christ. Do one-on-one Bible studies, share prayer
requests with each other, and even memorize
Scripture together. These relationships will be
some of the most meaningful and memorable on
your deployment.

ATTEND CHAPEL SERVICES AND BIBLE STUDIES (OR LISTEN TO AUDIO SERMONS)

The Bible is very clear that Christians must regularly worship through hearing the teaching of God's Word and by "encouraging one another" (Hebrews 10:25). If there simply is no chaplain or Christian leader to conduct either chapel services or Bible studies, think about loading up your MP3 player with sermons from a good preacher.

EVANGELIZE

Look for opportunities to make Christ known to those with whom you work. When I go on deployment, I have some of my best conversations about the Bible and Christ, probably because there is often a lot of "down time." We are not distracted by all the things at home. People are willing to think deeply and to discuss the claims of the Bible and of Christ. Be bold.

SERVE

As Christians, God has called us to serve, too. We are to serve others in the same way Christ served us in sacrificing himself for the sake of our good— the ultimate good of our salvation! In fact, Jesus has given us some very powerful illustrations of what our service should be like (John 13:1–17). We must not forget that when we serve others, looking out for the good of those around us, we provide the occasion for Christ to show himself through us (Matthew 5:14–16)!

Look for Evidence of God's Grace and Work around You

While on deployment, don't miss what God is doing through you and around you. Here are a few ways to look for evidence of his grace and work:

» Look to see God grow you spiritually.

» Look to see God deepen your love for Jesus.

» Look to see God grow your family and friends spiritually.

» Look to see God deepen your love for your family.

» Look to see a friend become a Christian.

» Look to see God answer prayers.

» Look to see God miraculously work in a situation.

When you begin looking for evidence of God's grace and work around you, he's more than happy to show you.

3. Apply the Gospel to the "Spiritual Difficulties"

The spiritual difficulties mentioned in Chapter 1 will be very real. Hopefully, however, by this point in the booklet you will have embraced a hope for your deployment, because of the gospel, what you have in Christ, all his benefits, and all God's precious promises toward you.

APPLYING THE GOSPEL TO THE SPIRITUAL DIFFICULTIES OF SEPARATION

Separation from Family And Friends

You now have the opportunity to explain to those closest to you your ultimate hope in Christ, all the promises God has given you, what God is doing, and how he can be trusted completely in this situation. Imagine if your family and friends all shared this same mindset: you would all rejoice that God knows exactly what he is doing, and that he has provided hope not only for you, but for your family and friends as well!

Separation from Your Church

It may be that members at your church are closer to you than your own family. Some of these members may never have experienced a person in their congregation leaving on a deployment. Some may need to hear how someone can truly have hope while deployed! Perhaps God could use you to help your church see the confidence we can have in Christ and his care for us even in a combat zone.

APPLYING THE GOSPEL TO THE SPIRITUAL DIFFICULTIES OF THE UNFAMILIAR AND UNKNOWN

Let what you have in the gospel of Christ instruct how you think about being away from your familiar environment and going into the unknown. But how do you do that? Think of it this way: our hearts reveal what we value, love, and live for. God is in the business of changing us at the heart level, so that we love the things he loves, have a holy dissatisfaction with the things he hates (2 Corinthians 3:18), we trust him, and we are happy in him alone, even during the challenges of the unfamiliar and unknown.

APPLYING THE GOSPEL TO THE SPIRITUAL DIFFICULTIES OF THE MILITARY ENVIRONMENT

When you face unimaginable combat experiences, do not forget what we have learned from the Bible about why the world is the way it is and the hope we have in Christ. When we face combat, we taste firsthand how broken our world is, and how wicked and rebellious people are toward God. When we see war, we see people at their ugliest, vying for power, control, money, and fame. We see men and women having no regard for the innocent and killing arbitrarily for their own ends. In fact, in war, we even see the ugliness that can come out of our own hearts. Yet it's this wicked world into which Christ came to save hopeless sinners like you, me, and even our enemies. We all desperately need the Savior.

Yes, let your heart break in times of war. Grieve and weep. This is not how the world should be. God created us to be in relationship with him, forever experiencing the pleasure of his presence. Yet as we saw in Chapter 2, we must live with the tension of being between the times of the garden and heaven. We know the end of the story. We know that God will put an end to this broken world and conquer his enemies (Revelation 20), but we also know that he has still given us responsibility to uphold justice and protect the innocent. We have a responsibility to fight well and to fight strongly. With Christ, we can also fight with absolute confidence.

In combat, there is no greater strength and hope you may cling to than all that Christ has given you in the gospel and his very precious promises. I cannot guarantee that you will not experience some very difficult things, including injury or death, but what I can guarantee is that, if you have Christ, Christ has you. Because of that, believers have the most hope on the battlefield. God will never leave us or forsake us. Even more, we have eternal life. Remember, in Christ, your soul is secure in God's hands forever. Heaven is already yours. Death is not your next chapter; life is. What better news when you are in the thick of battle? Praise God for the gospel. And remember the assurance found in Psalm 23:4:

> *Even though I walk through the valley of the shadow of death, I will fear no evil, for you are with me; your rod and your staff, they comfort me.*

CONCLUSION

If you haven't already heard those fateful words, "Pack your bags, we're going on deployment," then stick around the military a bit longer: you probably soon will. Either way, your next deployment can be successful now that you are armed with the hope of the gospel of Jesus Christ. For me to offer you anything other than the gospel to face this deployment would be like your armory offering you plastic guns and rubber bullets before combat. The gospel is the real thing, the true weapon; and it is highly effective. It is effective for the various spiritual difficulties you may face. It is effective in helping you to rightly understand why deployments even have to exist. It is effective on bad days. It is effective on good days. The gospel works, no matter the occasion.

In conclusion, let the gospel free you to have some fun on your deployment. Enjoy yourself, because God has rescued you in Christ and because of the unforgettable life experiences God will give you while abroad. Stay close to the Lord and continue to

> Grow in the grace and knowledge of our
> Lord and Saviour Jesus Christ.
>
> *(2 Peter 3:18)*

Personal Application Projects

Spiritual Pre-deployment Checklist

BEFORE YOU LEAVE ON DEPLOYMENT

Personal Preparation

» Remind yourself of the gospel: Psalm 103:11–12; Romans 6:9–11; Galatians 2:20; Colossians 2:13–14; 1 John 4:10.

» Spend time praying about your deployment, asking the Lord to prepare you spiritually for walking faithfully with him while you are away.

» Purchase a study Bible to use for personal study and devotion.

» Download several audio sermons onto your MP3 player (see the recommended resources in the "Where Can I Get More Help?" section at the back of this booklet).

» Download several Christian songs onto your MP3 player (see the recommended resources in the "Where Can I Get Further Help?" section at the back of this booklet).

» Choose a good Christian book to help you grow in your walk with Christ.

» Find a Bible reading plan to follow while you are deployed.

» Find a good devotional book to help you study a specific book in the Bible.

» Take a notebook so you can journal about the things the Lord has done for you.

Preparing with Your Family and Friends

» Go on multiple husband/wife/parent/friend dates to help your loved ones prepare for your absence. Pray with them.

» If married, help your spouse prepare for all the administrative and household responsibilities while you are gone.

» Go on daddy or mommy/child dates to ask your children how they are doing and to prepare them for your absence. Pray with them.

» Make numerous video recordings of yourself reading Scripture and praying for your friends or family, for them to watch while you're away.

» Before you go away, write letters to your spouse/children/parents/friends for them to open while you're away; pray with your spouse/children/parents/ friends.

» Husbands: pre-order flowers to be delivered to your wife a few times while you're away.

» Pre-order some toys to be delivered to your children while you're away.

Preparing with Your Church

» Meet with your pastor to share with him any fears you have. Ask him for his wisdom as to how you can make your deployment successful to the glory of God. Share with him the specific ways you need him to pray for you.

» If you are leaving your family behind, ensure that your church is willing to care for them spiritually while you're away.

» Ask your church for the opportunity to share with them what you will be doing on your deployment, providing them time to ask you questions. Also share with them ways you would like them to pray for you.

» Ask someone in your church to be an accountability partner for you while you're away. Look for someone who will regularly keep in contact with you, pray for you, and check how you are spiritually.

WHILE YOU ARE ON DEPLOYMENT

Personal Care

» Again, remind yourself of the gospel.

» Spend time regularly in prayer, asking the Lord to continue to help strengthen you spiritually to faithfully walk with him.

» Regularly read and study your Bible. Use your devotional materials.

» Choose a chapter in Scripture to memorize while you are deployed.

» Read the book you chose to bring.

» Listen to your sermons. Listen to good Christian music.

» Spend time journaling some of the ways in which the Lord has shown himself faithful.

» Find fellowship and accountability. Look for others who are reading their Bibles and desire Christian fellowship. Find out if there are any chapel services or Bible studies for you to attend.

» Make it a goal to share the gospel with ten people during your deployment.

Caring for Your Family, Friends, and Church

» Keep in touch! E-mail, phone, Skype, or do whatever you need to do to ensure that you are in regular communication with them.

» Be sure to speak hope to them, to pray with them, and to be honest about your fears or homesickness.

» Regularly look for ways to serve and love those around you with the joy you have in Christ.

Where Can I Get More Help?

BOOKS

Adsit, Chris, *The Combat Trauma Healing Manual: Christ-centered Solutions for Combat Trauma* (Newport News, VA: Military Ministry Press, 2007)

Demy, Timothy J., and Daryl, Charles J., *War, Peace, and Christianity: Questions and Answers from a Just-War Perspective* (Wheaton, IL: Crossway, 2010)

Dever, Mark, *The Gospel and Personal Evangelism* (Wheaton, IL: Crossway, 2007)

ESV Study Bible (Wheaton, IL: Crossway Bibles, 2007)

Lloyd-Jones, Martyn, *Why Does God Allow War?* (Wheaton, IL: Crossway, 2003)

MacArthur, John, *How to Study the Bible* (Chicago: Moody, 2009)

Packer, J. I., *Knowing God* (Downers Grove, IL: InterVarsity Press, 1993)

Stott, John R. W., *Basic Christianity* (Downers Grove, IL: Inter-Varsity Press, 1971)

Vincent, Milton, *A Gospel Primer for Christians: Learning to See the Glories of God's Love* (Bemidji, MN: Focus Publishing, 2008)

Whitney, Donald S., *Spiritual Disciplines for the Christian Life* (Colorado Springs: NavPress, 1991)

MILITARY MINISTRIES RESOURCES

Campus Crusade for Christ—Military Ministry: www.militaryministry.org

The Navigators Military Ministry: www.navigators.org/us/ministries/military

Cadence International Ministries to the Military: www.cadence.org

Officers' Christian Fellowship: www.ocfusa.org

AUDIO SERMON RESOURCES

Begg, Alistair: www.truthforlife.org

Dever, Mark: www.capitolhillbaptist.org/audio

Keller, Tim: http://sermons2.redeemer.com

MacArthur, John: www.gty.org/resources/sermons

Piper, John: www.desiringgod.org/resource-library/sermons/by-date

MUSIC RESOURCES

Getty Music: www.gettymusic.com

Indelible Grace: www.igracemusic.com

Sovereign Grace: http://sovereigngracemusic.org/sovereigngracemusic.org

BOOKS IN THE HELP! SERIES INCLUDE ...

Help! He's Struggling with Pornography
  ISBN 978-1-63342-003-8

Help! Someone I Love Has Been Abused
  ISBN 978-1-63342-006-9

Help! My Toddler Rules the House
  ISBN 978-1-63342-009-0

Help! Someone I Love Has Cancer
  ISBN 978-1-63342-012-0

Help! I Want to Change
  ISBN 978-1-63342-015-1

Help! My Spouse Has Been Unfaithful
  ISBN 978-1-63342-018-2

Help! I Have Breast Cancer
  ISBN 978-1-63342-024-3

Help! I'm a Slave to Food
  ISBN 978-1-63342-027-4

Help! My Teen Struggles With Same-Sex Attractions
  ISBN 978-1-63342-030-4

Help! She's Struggling With Pornography
  ISBN 978-1-63342-033-5

Help! I Can't Get Motivated
  ISBN 978-1-63342-036-6

Help! I'm a Single Mom
  ISBN 978-1-63342-039-7

Help! I'm Confused About Dating
  ISBN 978-1-63342-042-7

Help! I'm Drowning in Debt
  ISBN 978-1-63342-045-8

Help! My Teen is Rebellious
  ISBN 978-1-63342-048-9

Help! I'm Depressed
  ISBN 978-1-63342-051-9

Help! I'm Living With Terminal Illness
  ISBN 978-1-63342-054-0

Help! I Feel Ashamed
  ISBN 978-1-63342-057-1

Help! I Want to Understand Submission
  ISBN 978-1-63342-060-1

Help! Someone I Love Has Alzheimers
  ISBN 978-1-63342-063-2

Help! I Can't Handle All These Trials
  ISBN 978-1-63342-066-3

Help! I Can't Forgive
  ISBN 978-1-63342-069-4

Help! My Anger is Out of Control
  ISBN 978-1-63342-072-4

Help! My Friend is Suicidal
  ISBN 978-1-63342-075-5

Help! I'm in a Conflict
  ISBN 978-1-63342-078-6

(More titles in preparation)